I Love
Whales &
Dolphins

By Steve Parker

Miles Kelly

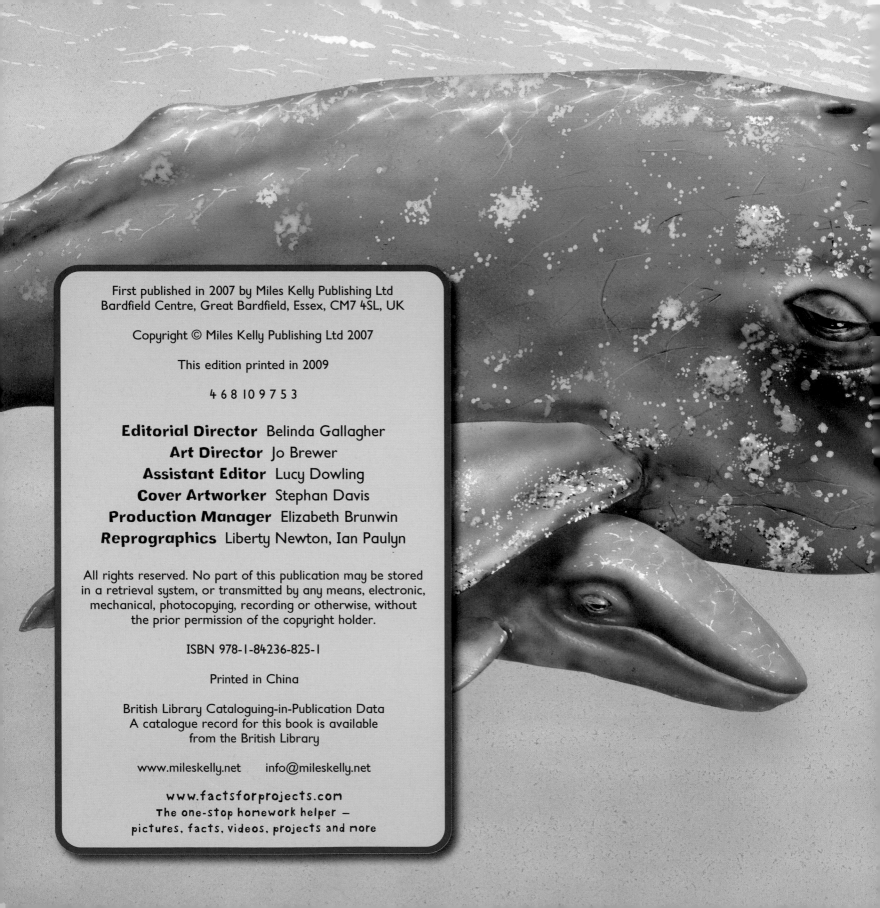

First published in 2007 by Miles Kelly Publishing Ltd
Bardfield Centre, Great Bardfield, Essex, CM7 4SL, UK

Copyright © Miles Kelly Publishing Ltd 2007

This edition printed in 2009

4 6 8 10 9 7 5 3

Editorial Director Belinda Gallagher
Art Director Jo Brewer
Assistant Editor Lucy Dowling
Cover Artworker Stephan Davis
Production Manager Elizabeth Brunwin
Reprographics Liberty Newton, Ian Paulyn

ISBN 978-1-84236-825-1

Printed in China

British Library Cataloguing-in-Publication Data
A catalogue record for this book is available
from the British Library

www.mileskelly.net   info@mileskelly.net

www.factsforprojects.com
The one-stop homework helper —
pictures, facts, videos, projects and more

Contents

Killer whale 4

Bottlenose dolphin 6

Atlantic spotted dolphin 8

Sperm whale 10

Dusky dolphin 12

Narwhal 14

Common dolphin 16

Grey whale 18

Humpback whale 20

Blue whale 22

Fun facts 24

Killer whale

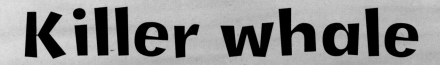

The killer whale is not actually a whale, but the biggest member of the dolphin family. It can kill and eat almost any creature in the sea, from a small fish to a large whale.

The fin on the back of whales and dolphins is called the dorsal fin. It helps them to stay upright in the water.

These dolphins live in large family groups called pods. Each pod is usually made up of 20 to 30 whales.

4

Some killer whales ride the surf onto the beach, grab a seal and wriggle back into the sea to eat it.

Hide and seek

The killer whale's colour helps it to hide in the sea. This means it can creep up and eat seals and sea lions.

As they circle their prey, killer whales 'talk' in clicks and squeaks.

Bottlenose dolphin

Bottlenose dolphins get their name because their snouts are shaped like round, hard bottles. These playful creatures race along at speeds of up to 50 kilometres an hour.

Once a dolphin catches its prey, it flicks the fish to the back of its mouth and swallows it whole.

A dolphin's smooth skin and shape helps it to swim quickly through water.

A dolphin has between 60 to 100 teeth, perfect for catching slippery fish.

Dolphins swim around small fish and gather them into tight groups called 'bait-balls.'

Click-click

Dolphins make clicking noises that bounce off fish and back to the dolphin. These help them to find their dinner.

Atlantic spotted dolphin

Dolphins have very sensitive skin. Atlantic spotted dolphins rub and stroke others in their group, or a partner during breeding time. A mother often rubs up against her baby to give it comfort and warmth.

Atlantic spotted dolphins do not have spots when they are born. These appear when they get older.

The tail of a dolphin is made up of two pieces. Each half is called a fluke.

Dolphins hold their breath while underwater. They come to the surface to breathe in air.

Different homes

Most dolphins live in the sea. The Amazon river dolphin however, lives in the rivers of South America.

To say hello, Atlantic spotted dolphins roll over and rub each other's bodies.

Sperm whale

The sperm whale is the largest hunter that has ever lived. It is found in all oceans, even cold Arctic waters, and is one of the deepest-diving whales. It can dive more than 3000 metres into the ocean.

Due to its enormous size, the sperm whale has the biggest brain of any animal.

This whale has a huge appetite. It hunts big fish and octopuses, but its favourite food is giant squid.

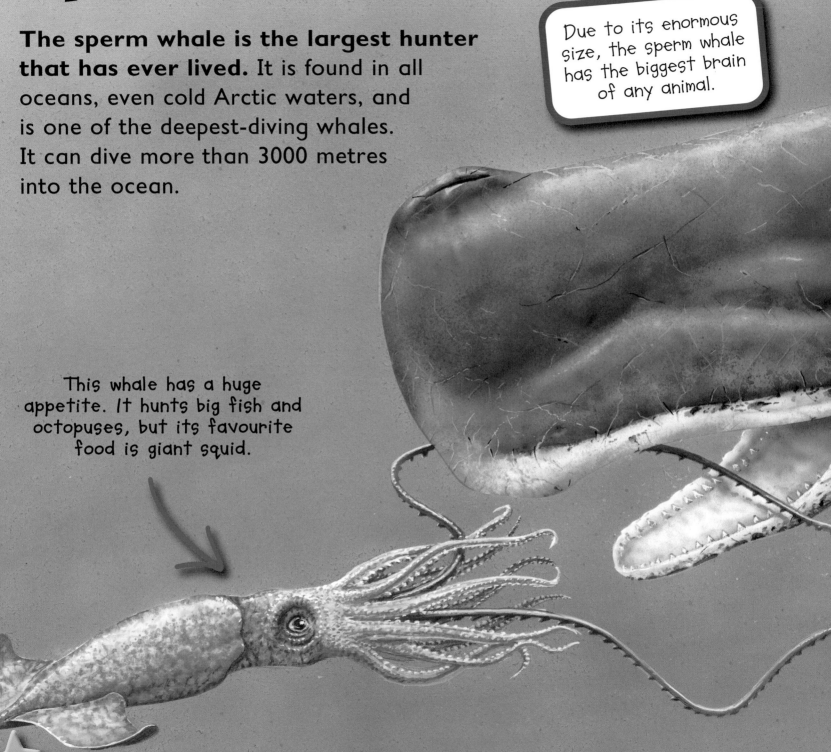

The sperm whale's back fin is just a small hump, with even smaller humps behind it.

There are about 50 teeth in the whale's lower jaw – but no teeth at all in its upper jaw.

Small giants
There are two other sperm whales. The pygmy sperm whale is medium-sized. The dwarf sperm whale is 'tiny', but twice as big as a person!

Dusky dolphin

Dolphins are very fast swimmers and can often be seen leaping above the waves. The dusky dolphin is one of the highest leapers, twisting and somersaulting before it splashes back into the sea.

To reach top speeds in the water, dolphins wave their tails up and down with great power.

Travelling in groups of up to 15 dolphins, these animals feed on squid and fish.

Dusky dolphins are very curious and like to swim and leap near boats.

Terrific teeth
Dolphins have lots of small, sharp teeth for spiking slippery fish and stabbing squirming squid.

These dolphins have been known to help people and other dolphins who are in trouble.

13

Narwhal

During the breeding season, some whales fight each other. Male narwhals show off their long tusks, waving them in the air at each other, and even using them like swords in a fight.

The narwhal's tusk is actually a very long, sharp tooth. It can grow up to 3 metres in length.

Using its bendy lips and tongue, the narwhal sucks in small fish from the ocean to eat.

Whitest whale

The narwhal's close cousin is called the beluga. This white whale is also very noisy — and it can make faces!

Male narwhals fight over females. The winner is then the most likely to mate with a female.

Common dolphin

Many kinds of dolphin live in large groups called schools. Common dolphins are colourful, with yellow patches along their sides and dark 'spectacles' around their eyes.

Dolphin bones

The skeleton of a whale or dolphin is made up of bones. They have no bones in the dorsal fin or the tail flukes.

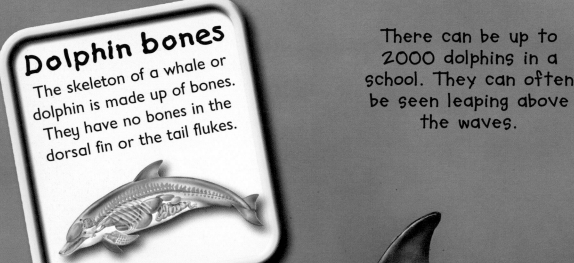

There can be up to 2000 dolphins in a school. They can often be seen leaping above the waves.

The common dolphin is very noisy. Its high-pitched squeak can sometimes be heard above the water.

If a group of
dolphins becomes
scared, they gather
closely together to
protect themselves.

Grey whale

Just like other mammals, whale and dolphin mothers give birth to babies and feed them on milk. The newborn grey whale is up to 5 metres in length and weighs more than half a tonne!

Grey whales poke their heads out of the water to look around. This is called spyhopping.

Pesky pests

Limpets and barnacles are small, shelled creatures. Usually they live on rocks, but some attach themselves to whales.

The mother helps her baby reach the surface of the water so that it can breathe air.

The young whale is called a calf. It stays with its mother for nine months, feeding on her milk.

The baby grey whale grows inside its mother's body for 13 months before it is born.

19

Humpback whale

Whales can sing! Their songs are squeaks, squeals and moans that travel through the water. The male humpback whale is one of the noisiest whales.

Whales can often be seen splashing backwards into the water. This is called breaching.

The male's song can last for 40 minutes or more. Then he sings it all again, for up to 20 hours!

The humpback's flippers are massive, up to 5 metres in length, with lumps along the front edge.

Sea snack

Humpback whales gulp in lots of water, trapping small animals inside their mouths to feed on.

Blue whale

The blue whale is the biggest animal in the world.
Yet its main food is tiny, shrimplike creatures called krill.
Each one is smaller than your finger. The blue whale eats
more than 4 tons of krill every day.

The blue whale is about 33 metres in length and weighs 190 tonnes.

The blue whale can make a grunting sound that is louder than a space rocket taking off!

As the blue whale dives into the water, its tail sticks high into the air.

The tongue of a blue whale is so big that over 50 people would be able to stand on it.

Whale out of water

Instead of teeth, many whales have long strips of a tough, springy substance called baleen.

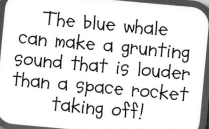

Fun facts

Killer whale One of the fastest swimmers, the killer whale can reach speeds of up to 55 kilometres an hour.

Bottlenose dolphin These dolphins can live to be 50 years old.

Blue whale The heart of the blue whale is the size of a small family car.

Sperm whale A sperm whale has huge teeth. A single tooth weighs as much as a bag of sugar.

Grey whale These whales are often found in shallow water and enjoy swimming in the surf.

Common dolphin This is one of the most playful dolphins. It loves to turn somersaults in the air.

Humpback whale These whales travel on long journeys so they can give birth to their young in warmer waters.

Narwhal
Sometimes narwhals may get trapped beneath ice at the water's surface. They then have to head-butt the ice to make a breathing hole.

Dusky dolphin Once one dusky dolphin begins to leap out of the water, others in the group quickly follow.

Atlantic spotted dolphin Other names for the Atlantic spotted dolphin are the spotted porpoise and the long snouted dolphin.